Presentation Perfect

Presentation Perfect

How to excel at business presentations,
meetings and public speaking

Alastair Grant

The Industrial Society

First published 1997 by
The Industrial Society
Robert Hyde House
48 Bryanston Square
London W1H 7LN
Telephone: 0171 479 2000

© The Industrial Society 1997

ISBN 1 85835 493 5

**British Library Cataloguing-in-Publication Data.
A catalogue record for this book is available from the
British Library.**

**Library of Congress
Cataloguing-in-Publication
Data on File**

Typeset by: The Midlands Book Typesetting Co.
Printed by: Galliard (Printers) Ltd
Cover design: Rhodes Design

The Industrial Society is a Registered Charity No. 290003

Acknowledgements

When my firm, Grant Pearson Brown & Co, first established itself in 1993 one of its first projects was to design and run advanced presentation skills courses for The Industrial Society – the UK's leading provider of training, specialising in, amongst other areas, communication and presentation skills.

These courses have now become a regular feature of our life, but the structure and content of the courses have evolved over time. This evolution has come about as a result of feedback received from course attendees and from critical, but constructive, comments from the Industrial Society, in particular Chrissie Wright and Patricia Adams.

When I was asked by Chrissie if we would like to write a book on what we had developed, I was delighted to accept.

I am grateful to various people, both within The Industrial Society and my own firm, for their input. In particular, within The Society, Chrissie Wright who approached me in the first place and Susannah Lear who charmingly encouraged my efforts. Within my own firm, Nigel Brown, Tim Corry, Lia Nathans and Ian McDougall, who have all made valuable contributions. My thanks also to Caroline Cowie who swept up behind and put the book into some sort of shape.

Alastair Grant
Grant Pearson Brown & Co

Grant Pearson Brown & Co are based in London with affiliates in Australia, North America and Hong Kong. They help companies with a variety of communication skills as well as providing assistance for specific events including conference presentations, business pitches, and companies going through management change.

e-mail:agrant@gpbuk.demon.co.uk

Contents

Introduction

Professionals need many skills to be effective. An accountant has to handle figures, a teacher has to handle people. Few of us would get very far if we could not communicate well. In order to negotiate, present, persuade, inform and interact we all need to speak effectively.

One of the characteristics of many able people is their ability to communicate successfully. What links Winston Churchill, Martin Luther King, Patrick Moore, John Harvey-Jones and Anna Ford? – they can all speak effectively.

This book aims to help all levels of staff, but particularly those in senior management positions, who must rise above normal conversational skills to perform effectively in meetings, negotiations, conferences, briefings and business pitches; occasions which, for the purposes of this book, we will group under the generic heading "presentations".

Some of us are born with a strong and charismatic style. Being outgoing and able, we naturally become good speakers. Others are low key, understated and dread public performance. Can such people become effective presenters? The answer is an emphatic "Yes"! The ability to speak and present effectively does not stem from inherent talent alone, it is a skill that can be learnt and developed - even quiet, understated people can communicate with force and persuasion.

This book is a toolbox of ideas and insights that have been tried and tested by many, and have been found not only to be practical but also to have helped people *actually change their behaviour*. The toolbox divides into three main compartments – physical tools, intellectual tools and interactive tools.

Physical tools – In this first compartment we consider "physical tools" such as pace, eye contact, and being in control. These are tools that allow people to come across to an audience with greater confidence and conviction. These tools are not easy to use and, as with any physical skill, such as learning to play golf or a musical instrument, they require practice, observation and critique. A book can only take you so far. Some of the physical skills we write about here are the same as those that might be taught at Drama School.

Intellectual tools – In the second compartment we consider "intellectual tools" in other words, the content of a speech or presentation. We also consider how to structure this content in such a way that it will be accessible and stimulating for your audience. Here the skills of a journalist are more relevant.

Interactive tools - You may speak fluently and have a well constructed message but then blow it all because you mishandle questions from your audience. The reverse is also true. Many presenters come to life in the question and answer session. The "tools" required for these interactive sessions are considered in the third, and final, compartment.

We are often, and rightly, asked the simple question: "How do you measure someone's performance when making a presentation?" This, of course, is a subjective issue. However, an audience can measure performance in two areas. These translate into two fundamental objectives that need to be achieved.

First, there is a need for the presenter's message to come across. This sounds pretty obvious, but it is not uncommon after a presentation for an audience to be unable to recall the key points with any clarity. We set a simple test. Can the listener retell the presenter's story to a third party later on? We call this the "Third Party Test".

Second, there is a need for the presenter's personality to come across. Audiences always make a subjective judgement on the presenter. Do I trust this person? Does this person appear to know what they are talking about? Do I get a sense of this person's integrity and enthusiasm? Is this person someone I would like to do business with? Again, we regularly see presenters who fail to convince through *not* projecting their personality. This is not some macho issue; even quiet, introverted people can be very effective.

If you really accept these two objectives, then you have taken a significant step. What you are in effect saying is "nothing else matters" in terms of making a presentation or formal speaking in any business situation. In other words, if you scratch your nose, put the overhead on upside down or talk with the wrong accent, it really doesn't matter as long as people can remember the essence of your message and gain a positive impression of you, the personality.

I well remember Ken Livingstone speaking at a government management college. Most of the audience were not left wing and anticipated that they would probably disagree with what Ken had to say. However, without bravado or hectoring, Ken had a profound effect on us. We all found him to be highly engaging and persuasive. (Although we did not agree with all his ideas, we nonetheless were persuaded about some by the strength of his arguments and his personality.)

Chapter 1 – contents

Physical skills

Quiz

Answer the following questions.

Q1. In the Introduction, we outlined two key objectives of presentation:

● That the presenter's message comes across, and
● That his or her personality comes across.

Which of these two objectives do you consider to be the more important, or are both equally important?

Q2. Who do you consider to be a good presenter?

Q3. Can you identify a situation when the presenter did very well in one aspect but failed completely in another? Did it actually matter?

See page 9 for our comments.

Introduction

This chapter dives headlong into the physical tool box and explores the concept of a "conversational style". In particular:

Pace – Telling people to slow down is unhelpful advice. Vitality and energy can be put across when the presenter says something rapidly. Similarly, telling people to speed up is not always good advice. Sometimes it is important to slow down, to add emphasis. Pace, however, is not simply about the rate of word delivery, it is also about variation, emphasis and pausing. Pausing is inherently difficult to do. It is not instinctive, particularly when people are nervous. In this chapter we explain the "Time Distortion Effect".

Eye contact – Conventional wisdom suggests that you should achieve plenty of eye contact, the more the better. We explain how eye contact works in a positive well-conducted conversation between two people.

When presenting most people display a "dismissive style" instead of an engaging conversational style.

Conversation

Our definition of a positive "conversational style" as opposed to a "presentational style" is quite complex and contains a number of paradoxes. The case study below illustrates the difference between *conversation* and *presentation*.

Case study

The staff and students of a government management college I formerly attended expected to hear two presentations that morning. The first was on the structure of the Civil Service. It failed to excite much anticipation. The second was on Britain's intelligence services. This sounded more like it.

The senior civil servant arrived ... late. He leaned over the podium clutching some scruffy, pencil written notes. "Sorry I'm late" he said, "I was held up. I had to call by Number 10 on the way here. Rather than give you lots of detail on the Civil Service I thought I'd tell you about my meeting." We all leaned forward in our chairs and listened to his account of what he and the Prime Minister of the day had discussed.

Case study

By contrast, the second presentation was a flop. There were many well prepared slides. All very slick, but very dull.

Our expectations were reversed. The senior civil servant, a busy man, held a conversation with us. He told us stories that bordered on the indiscreet. His aim was to give us an insight into the relationship between politicians and civil servants. The intelligence services speaker, on the other hand, delivered a presentation to us. He dumped far too much detail on us - he and his message faded rapidly.

Key features

Being conversational sounds easy enough, but it's not that simple in practice!

There are a number of reasons why people become stiff and over-presentational in a formal situation. It isn't just a matter of nerves but more the way the brain is conditioned to work.

So what is conversation anyway? And why is it different to presentation? We can identify a number of features in a conversational style.

First, in conversation, people tend not to speak in perfect sentences. They punctuate what they say in quite a different way to how they would punctuate what they write. The mistake people often make in presentations is to use formal language for the eye and not the ear. The ear is conditioned to informal language, which is colloquial.

Second, they pause all over the place! They pause to:

- Think.
- Allow the other person to respond.
- Seek an effect.
- Emphasise with silence.

Third, they regularly seek acknowledgement of the listener. In effect, their eye contact is saying, "Did you get that?" or "OK?" We call this an "engaging style". The listener has a certain amount of control over any presenter because if the listener fails to respond the presenter starts to feel uncomfortable. People use an engaging style instinctively in conversation but tend not to use it when presenting or speaking formally as their brain is looking, and thinking, ahead.

Finally, in conversation people tend to get inflection, tone and timbre about right, but when presenting they use less expression and become more measured and flat.

Tools from the physical tool box

So much for the theory, what about the practice? What tools can we pull out of the physical box to improve our powers of presentation? Let's look in more detail at pace and eye contact.

Pace

This is the first, and most basic, building block. We often hear comments like "You're going too fast" or "slow down" as an inexperienced or nervous individual gallops through his talk or presentation at break neck speed. The well intentioned adviser is asking the presenter to talk more slowly or, to put it another way, to slow down the rate of word delivery (apparently, 120 words a minute is the norm).

The advice is wrong! Merely to slow down the rate of word delivery is to stultify and diminish life, vitality and spark. Good presenters often do speak quite quickly but they have the ability to pause and vary their pace.

Two issues arise out of this which impact directly on the presenter's key objectives – to convey both their message and their personality:

● In terms of conveying the message, presenters/speakers should make use of pauses. After all, listeners not only have to listen but also to *think*. (When reading, do you ever realise that you have just read a paragraph but were thinking about something completely different and so haven't taken the meaning in? You then have to reread.) If the pace is too quick then the listener either tracks the speaker but fails to register the meaning, or takes time out to think about the meaning but then has to rejoin the speaker knowing they have missed part of the talk. *A major reason why messages fail to be remembered by listeners is because speakers do not give them time to think.*

● In terms of conveying personality, speakers need to vary their pace or rate of word delivery. Passion, commitment and enthusiasm rarely come across if a presentation is entirely delivered at a slow, mechanical pace. They also need to talk with expression and get the emphasis right.

Eye contact

On some presentation skills courses, delegates are encouraged to increase eye contact with the audience. However, this rather misses the point. Too much eye contact can appear aggressive and it certainly doesn't work well in every cultural context.

Typically, people who read from a script, or use bullet points or visuals as a prompt, tend to look at their audience in the middle of an idea and then plunge down to search for a new piece of information. People do this because they are concerned about the future. The brain wants to know what's happening next. This is another aspect of a "presentational style".

We recommend you cultivate two habits:

● Pause and look at your audience before you begin a key point. You appear to be thinking and this lends a certain gravitas to your manner. We call this the "I am thinking" pause.
● Pause at the end of the thought or idea and look at the individual or group. This is the "Did you get that?" emphasis. (It's the same pause as mentioned above when allowing time for the message to be processed.)

What goes wrong?

Relying solely on instinct doesn't work. You may well accept our argument about the superior merits of being conversational but the problem is we are all sometimes nervous or under pressure when presenting. Our instincts for being conversational desert us as our brain is more concerned with other issues – usually what to say next!

The time distortion effect

When we are nervous our sense of timing can become distorted. Pausing for one second feels much longer. If we lose our place in a script, we feel disorientated as we scramble to find the place. The audience may never notice that one second gap but for us it feels like an eternity. Experienced presenters get used to this phenomenon, but only up to a point. You can't turn off the adrenalin, but it certainly helps to get used to silence.

Summary

Conversation vs presentation

We have a paradox. This book is all about helping you to present more effectively but here is the paradox – *you will be more effective if you are conversational and not presentational.* Being conversational, being yourself, means:

- Varying your pace. Quick to be exciting and slow for emphasis.
- Using expression and inflection, but don't ham it up!
- Pausing before you begin a key point. The "I am thinking" pause.
- Deliberately pausing to allow messages to sink home. This same pause allows you to provide emphasis and be engaging with eye contact. "Did you get that?" Remember, it's not instinctive!

Quiz answers

A1. It depends. Opinions vary considerably as to which objective is the more important. It is often a combination of the two. If you are listening to the weather forecast then you are seeking specific information and the personality of the presenter is of no significance, but in any situation where the presenter is seeking to persuade then personality becomes pre-eminent. We can certainly see situations where the personality wins the day despite the message being forgotten. (See **A.3** below.)

A2. When asked to name a good presenter, most people come up with a TV personality. Many are indeed very good presenters, but they operate in a highly visual medium and often have the qualities of a showman and entertainer. In other fields politicians are often quoted. Sadly, businessmen in the UK hardly get a rating except for John Harvey-Jones and Richard Branson. In America men like Lee Iacocca, former Chief Executive Officer of the Chrysler Corporation, and Bill Gates of Microsoft get more visibility.

My firm has its own favourites, for example, Winston Churchill and Alistair Cooke. With Churchill, it is not just his heroic famous wartime speeches which attract our approval, but his masterly command of the spoken language which even now, some 50 years or so later, still has freshness and clarity.

Alistair Cooke might seem a curious choice, but he is an example of someone who speaks well but isn't often seen as he usually "appears" on radio. Cooke can talk about complex issues in a conversational way so that the listener finds it easy to pick up the general argument, and remember it later.

A3. Many people can identify such a situation.

Recently, whilst helping at an internal conference, I listened to speakers all day. Later everyone sat down to dinner. Then it was the turn of the newly appointed chairman to speak. He spoke well but it is doubtful that

Quiz answers the delegates, with a few post-dinner glasses of wine inside them, picked up many specifics. What they did pick up, however, was that their new chairman was passionately interested in the success of the company and appeared to have a very good grasp of what was going on.

Personality won the day even if the message could not be retold later.

Chapter 2 – contents

Script reading skills

Quiz   Do you agree or disagree with these statements?

S1.   Reading from a script is the quickest way to put an audience to sleep.

S2.   I don't know my subject well so I think it best to stick to a script.

S3.   I want to speak faultlessly on important occasions so should use a script.

S4.   Reading from a script is easy to do.

See page 20 for our comments.

Introduction

The vast majority of speakers dislike or refuse to use a script. It is hardly surprising as we can all conjure up images of tedious conference speakers droning on devoid of personality. Yet some of the world's best presenters have followed scripts. For example, Churchill and Alistair Cooke.

Why use a script?

A script is a very useful tool to pull out of the box on certain occasions, particularly if:

- You wish to choose your words with care.
- Your words may have legal implications or the press are in attendance.
- You want to speak for a certain length of time.
- You haven't had time to rehearse well enough to be able to speak ad-lib.
- You are nervous. If you are feeling nervous and keyed up it can be extremely comforting and helpful to know that all you have to do is to follow your script.

This chapter explains some simple techniques that can make speakers engaging and convincing whilst reading from a script word for word. The chapter is not intended to persuade the reader to use scripts but rather to highlight the fact that scripts can be a useful tool when there is a need to be precise, on time and unambiguous.

There are two key requirements for success.

First, the text has to be written in language fit for the *ear* and not the *eye*. Not surprisingly, when writing most people try to construct sentences that are grammatically correct. But the ear doesn't care too much about this! It is much more interested in your ideas and being able to understand them! Look at the two examples below. Can you spot the difference between *ear* and *eye* language?

Example 1 Europe's economic and demographic patterns may seem uncongenial for private equity investment. There is little doubt that high taxation, uncompetitive wage costs, over-regulation of labour markets and the ageing of the population will constrain economic growth. However, some likely responses to these problems may lead to major structural changes to Europe's economies and capital markets, and these changes will create major new opportunities for investors in private equity.

Example 2   I have three images of cyclists.

My first is of families at weekends in brightly coloured, Dan Dare helmets, others on strange looking machines in black lycra shorts.

My second image is of courier bikers weaving through city traffic, mobiles at the ready, and using their own version of the highway code!

But it's my third image that I want to sell to you today. People using bikes instead of cars to get to work. Using bikes to do their business.

Second, the layout of the script has to be clear and logical. Compare the two passages above. Which is easier to read?

Reading techniques

Almost without exception, when someone reads from a script they tend to look up in the middle of a sentence and plunge down at the end. The reason for this is simple enough. They want to know what lies ahead. The brain is concerned about the future, it needs security.

We will now consider some techniques to overcome this tendency.

The Kissinger

The first technique reverses this tendency by asking the reader to look down at a sentence and read it out without looking at the audience at all until the last three words or so. As the reader gets to the end so he looks up at the audience and, finally, holds a pause with eye contact. This is the eye contact pause that provides the "Did you get that?" emphasis. It gives an impression of conviction and force. It is also engaging and conversational. This technique was apparently given to US statesmen to use some twenty years ago and became known as "The Kissinger" for obvious reasons.

Exercise

Read through the passage below. Now imagine you are delivering the text to an audience and read through the passage again. Notice how you try to eye ball the audience in the middle of each phrase and then dive back at the end?

Now do it again, but this time make a point of coming up for the last three or four words of each phrase. Imagine you are looking at the audience and feel very strongly about what you are saying.

"Safety is the prime concern ... Too many people are worried they might get clobbered by a truck or even a motorist opening their door without looking.

It is safety that probably prevents more people from taking to their bikes. Some journeys will never be suitable for the bike, but many are.

What we must do is try to create safe conditions to encourage more people to get on their bike!"

The Kissinger technique is easy to do and very effective, but it must be used sparingly lest it becomes monotonous or contrived.

If you decide to read no further in this chapter then we would recommend, and reinforce, one message – that, when using a script, you highlight two or three key phrases on each page and commit to a Kissinger at that point.

The diagram opposite illustrates a Kissinger. As with the other two diagrams illustrating reading techniques in this chapter, the horizontal axis represents time and the vertical axis shows where your eyes are. The parallel vertical bars represent the area where you pause and look at your audience.

Most people have little difficulty with looking down at a script and then swooping up to connect with the audience, but now on to more challenging techniques.

The Kissinger

1. Look down at script – read
2. Start to look up but continue talking
3. Pause with eye contact "Did you get that?"

The Bite

The next technique, which we call "The Bite", can produce feelings of discomfort, disorientation and a general feeling that the wool is being pulled over the reader's eyes! Here's how to do it.

● Look down at your script and take a mental "snapshot" of three or four words. (This should be achieved in a split second.)
● Look up at the audience, maintaining eye contact for about a second, and say nothing.
● Then say the three or four words that you picked up with as much conviction as you can muster!
● Finally, pause, maintaining eye contact.

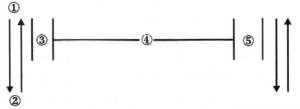

The Bite

1. Look down at script
2. Snapshot – grab about three words and look up
3. Pause – "thinking"
4. Say the words
5. Pause with eye contact "Did you get that?"

This Bite technique forms the basis of oratory. Three or four words, followed by eye contact and a pause, can be dramatic and powerful. Your words hang in the air and are absorbed in silence by the audience. You appear to speak with complete conviction. This technique can still be conversational though. Churchill in the US Congress said the following in Bite mode:

"By the way// I cannot help reflecting// that if my father had been born American// and my mother English// instead of the other way around// I might have gotten there// on my own."

The Bite technique is difficult to do and most people find it rather stilted. Unless you are into oratory then this technique should be used selectively in case your audience think you have gone into politics! However, even though this technique is difficult, don't be tempted not to use it at all. This technique can raise the level of your presentational game as you appear to be conversational yet persuasive. Also, it is not at all obvious to your audience that you are using a script. The words that come out of your mouth appear to be coming freshly brewed from your brain and not from some dull old script!

The Eyescan

The final technique is called "The Bathtub" or "Eyescan". This technique is a mixture of the Bite and the Kissinger. To use this technique you begin in just the same way as you would with a Bite.

- Glance down at the script and latch on to a phrase (three or four words).
- Glance up and do a "thinking" pause.
- Deliver your point, but before you run out of memory, casually glance down and reconnect with your script.
- Keep reading whilst looking down at the script and then come up and pause like you would with a Kissinger.

Once mastered, the Eyescan proves popular, but beware! If all you do is Eyescans then you will appear contrived and dull. You must be brave and commit yourself to doing some Bites.

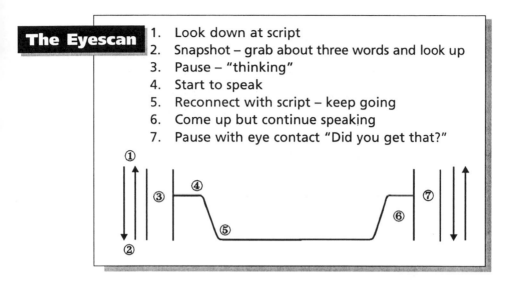

The Eyescan
1. Look down at script
2. Snapshot – grab about three words and look up
3. Pause – "thinking"
4. Start to speak
5. Reconnect with script – keep going
6. Come up but continue speaking
7. Pause with eye contact "Did you get that?"

Health warning!

Too many techniques are bad for you.

Our advice is to use these techniques selectively and build up confidence. If you try too hard, you will become pre-occupied and your performance will suffer.

At least commit yourself to a couple of Kissingers on a page of script - it might be helpful to highlight them. Also, make sure your script is produced in the right font size for comfort and is written in easy-to-read, conversational language.

Summary

- There are occasions when reading from a script will be the best way to get your message across.
- The techniques outlined above are easy enough to handle individually, but difficult to handle simultaneously. Build up your skills slowly.
- Avoid doing everything with a Kissinger or an Eyescan. You must be brave and attempt some conversational Bites.

- Scripts must be written in *ear* language.
- Stick to your script and avoid the temptation to ad-lib. Remember Gerald Ratner (of Ratners, jewellers), who ad-libbed so disastrously about the poor quality of both his company's products and customers!

Quiz answers

A1. Disagree. Reading from a script can be boring if the reader fails to be conversational and, as a result, their personality gets lost. However, by using technique and stage craft you can transform your performance.

A2. Agree. It's a good move to follow a script or well-written notes.

A3. Agree. We advise people to follow their script on important occasions. Gerald Ratner didn't, to his cost.

A4. Disagree. Reading from a script requires a high degree of skill to make the message come across well.

Chapter 3 – contents

Using notes

Do you agree or disagree with these statements?

S1. If I use notes I will give the impression I don't know my subject.

S2. I write down my notes but somehow I don't really follow them.

S3. I believe the best way to use notes is to put bullet points up on a slide so the listeners can *see* as well as *hear* them.

See page 28 for our comments.

Introduction

Most of us use notes as a means of reminding ourselves of the main points of a speech. Some of us actually follow our notes; others use them as a safety net. We encourage people to use notes in a more disciplined way than they are used to because we find that, far from losing face or appearing to be incompetent, people who follow their notes tend to be brief and focused. By using the skills outlined in chapters one and two they can project their personality as well.

Using notes correctly can save a huge amount of time, both for the presenter who no longer rambles as he tries to recall the next point, and for the listener whose time is used efficiently.

The problem

Using notes well sounds fine in theory but typically, in practice, presenters:

● Don't really follow their notes once they get going.
● Tend to ramble and add extra information.
● Become presentational rather than engaging in a positive conversational style.
● Don't really believe they need to use notes as they know the subject well.

So what goes wrong?

People mishandle notes for a variety of reasons, many of which they are quite unaware of. These reasons are examined in more detail below.

Notes are badly written

The problem
A presenter often writes notes as a mind clearing exercise. This is all very well, but these notes tend to make little sense once the presenter actually starts to speak. The brain takes over.

The solution
It takes skill to write notes. The presenter has to make sure the layout is clear, the font legible and that he selects appropriate key words (and omits what can be safely left out).

The wimp factor

The problem

We are always impressed by people who speak brilliantly without a note or prompt in sight and aspire to do the same ourselves. As a result, some of us try to do without any notes at all, "Look Mum, no hands!" Some of us continue to use notes but try to hide them away as though embarrassed to be seen using them.

The solution

If you are indeed brilliant, or have the time to memorise and rehearse your lines, then you may judge the effort of not using notes worthwhile. However, in most situations, far from being seen to be inadequate or a "wimp" for using notes, people are impressed that you have taken the time to prepare. Some presenters reduce their notes to tiny cards. Cards have the advantage of being portable but they can be rather fiddly to use in practice. Why not be happy to have your notes on a bold piece of A4 paper, perhaps on a clipboard if you are walking about? (You will see people like Jeremy Paxman doing just that on some of his shows.)

Notes aren't considered necessary

The problem

Many people believe they don't need to use notes, but they are missing the point. The presenter is not there to demonstrate his vast knowledge but to be clear and intelligible to the listener.

The solution

Although you may know a subject well, you can increase the clarity of your message and be more persuasive by following notes. Putting this realisation into practice can pay tremendous dividends.

Notes are not followed

The problem

The presenter has notes but tends not to follow them once underway. This happens to most of us. We fall into the trap of *talking whilst thinking*. Typically, we use the notes to kick off an idea but then our brain cannot resist adding extra information. We ramble on or enthusiastically embroider the original idea. Eventually, we end up saying something that is weak and inconsequential. We fail to hold pauses or be engagingly conversational.

We fail to follow prepared notes for a number of reasons, including:

● We rely solely on our memory. It never occurs to us to actually follow our notes.
● Once committed to using our brain we become focused on remembering the next thing to say and so keep talking until the next idea can be conjured up.
● We fear silence so talk to fill what we believe to be an unacceptable gap.

The solution

Training your brain to follow notes is by no means easy. It is a skill and requires practice. The following tips may help you:

● Use the techniques of script reading to be more succinct and conversational. If you have difficulty in concluding an idea then try looking down at your notes as you speak but come up and pause. In other words, do a Kissinger or Eyescan. Of course, you can do Bites as well but the point here is to train your brain to follow the notes more closely.
● Use your notes not only to launch a new idea but also to finish, or draw a line, under one idea before proceeding to the next. This will help you move the argument forward in a concise and structured way.

Case study   My firm once had a client who was excellent at his job of asset management but quite incapable of communicating his message to other people as he could not control the flow of his ideas. His firm could not put him in front of prospects. The remedy was to persuade him to follow his notes rigidly, to the extent of actually ticking off each point as he made it in front of a prospect. The effect was dramatic. He was under control and the listener had a chance of understanding his clever ideas.

Thoughts are run together

The problem

The presenter moves from one idea to the next without returning to his notes. As a result, the listener has difficulty in following the argument except with hindsight. The act of pausing and then looking down at the next note acts like a punctuation marker – "Something new is coming up".

The solution

As stated above, be more disciplined in following your notes.

Summary

- Write good, clear notes in the first place.
- Make an effort to follow your notes.
- Use the techniques of script reading to make sure you follow the notes yet remain conversational.
- Avoid "talking whilst thinking".
- Avoid running thoughts together.
- Keep practising, it's not easy.

Quiz answers **A1.** Disagree. In almost every case being seen to refer to notes has a positive effect, it gives the impression of having taken trouble to prepare.

A2. Agree. Most people are not conditioned to following their notes in detail as they prefer to follow what their memory tells them.

A3. Disagree. Many presenters do this but it can act as a distraction as the listener thinks about a different point to the one being discussed and you, the personality, can be diminished by making the slides the focus of attention.

Chapter 4 – contents

Content and structure

Quick planner quiz You have an important presentation to make next week. You know the subject quite well. How do you prepare? Answer the questions of this quick planner quiz.

Q1. Why are you doing the presentation? Are you hoping to inform? Persuade? Encourage dialogue?

Q2. Can you, in 20 seconds, write down the most important point you want your audience to remember?

Q3. Do you want them to remember anything else, if so, what?

Q4. How can you illustrate your key points? Would you use visual aids or vivid examples?

Q5. Is what is clear to you abstract to the listener?

Q6. Will you rely on memory, notes, visual aids or a script to make sure you keep to the point?

Q7. Will you use any handouts?

If you can answer these simple questions then you are half way there!

Introduction

This chapter considers the content of a speech or presentation. The majority consists of general advice on such issues as how to identify your key message, and how to know what information to put in and what to leave out. It also offers advice on how to structure this content for maximum effect.

The chapter concludes with a detailed look at the whole presentation process – from the moment you have a date in your diary to the delivery of the presentation.

Content

Content is all about *message* rather than *delivery*. When asked to present, people often see their objective at two different levels. The headline level will refer to the most obvious objective – you need to speak to an individual or group about a certain topic. The second, below-the-line, level will refer to a more underlying or subliminal objective.

For a start you are on show. You want to impress and do well for your own self-esteem. More than this, you may wish to persuade your audience to buy into an idea. Of course, the headline objective and the subliminal one may be exactly the same and obvious to all. However, it is important to establish why you are making a presentation and what you hope to achieve before preparing your presentation in detail.

Six reasons to present

We can identify six primary reasons to present:
- To brief (updating or informing people).
- To instruct (informing or teaching your audience).
- To inspire (inspiring or motivating your audience).
- To advocate (convincing or selling a point of view to an audience).

- To stimulate (stimulating discussion and debate with your audience).
- To gratify (entertaining or amusing your audience).

Obviously, a presentation could combine most, or all, of these six objectives – convincing through stimulating debate, instructing in an entertaining way, and then inspiring the audience to follow up on the message.

Getting started

Problems

The first hurdle a presenter may face when trying to organise content could be either:
- Having a surplus of information and not knowing where to start, or
- Being unsure they have enough information of the right sort. They may also suffer from writer's block.

Solutions

The 20 second rule

A good starting point to clear the mind in either situation is to take a clean sheet of paper and give yourself 20 seconds to write down the single most important fact/idea/message you want your audience to remember.

One way to help focus on what this might be is to imagine that a fire has started in the room where you are giving your presentation. Out of everything you might have said to your audience you only have 20 seconds before your audience have to leave the room. What would you say? This becomes your "key key point".

The 60 second rule

Spend another 60 seconds writing down the three or so most important ideas or facts that support or reinforce your key key point. These now become your "key points".

From this start there are a number of ways to extend this process. Here are three:

- Divide a sheet of A4 paper vertically into two columns. Into the left hand column brainstorm your ideas in random fashion without any concern about order or relative importance. Indeed, you may put down ideas which you don't intend to use immediately. Now rearrange those ideas on the right hand side in a logical order.
- Mindmap from the centre. We don't have space here to explain the technique of mindmapping in great detail. The idea is to start from the centre of the page, jotting down your thoughts, and work outwards. Each key theme becomes a spoke or branch that radiates out from the centre. As ideas occur you add to existing branches or start a new branch. The advantage of this system is that it is not linear so you are not inhibited by a list mentality and you can always find space to add more information.
- Simply start writing! This sounds unhelpful advice, but I am surprised at the number of people who find that the act of writing seems to release hidden thoughts in their brain.

Writer's block

Despite going through the above process your brain has stalled and refuses to deliver the goods. If this is the case, you may find considering the following points helpful in unblocking the jam:

- Position – what is the current position?
- Problems – what problems do you seek to discuss?
- Possibilities – what options are open?
- Proposal – what are you hoping will be done?

Of course, not every talk can be grouped under these four points, nor should each point be given equal weight. However, we find that many topics do quite easily fall under these broad headings.

Practical points

Limit your information

A constant criticism we receive about business presentations is that speakers tend to say too much — there is an overload of information.

Our advice is to limit your presentation to a few key points to ensure that your listeners remember them all. The fewer ideas you give to your listeners the greater the chance that they will remember more of what you have said. By limiting the number of ideas you have a better chance of achieving one of the two primary objectives of presentation - making your message memorable.

Consider the following:

Question — If during a presentation someone was to give you 100 facts or ideas, in percentage terms, how many might you remember?

Answer - 10% or so?

Question - If during a presentation someone was to give you ten facts or ideas, in percentage terms, how many might you remember?

Answer - 40 or 50%?

Question - If during a presentation someone was to give you three facts or ideas, in percentage terms, how many might you remember?

Answer - 100%?

The fewer the number of ideas you give your audience to remember the greater the proportion they are likely to remember.

This point is particularly relevant when presenting to groups of 20 or more people as there is likely to be less interaction. When talking to an individual or a small group it is possible to get more points across because a dialogue can be started which allows the speaker to get feedback on what the listeners are picking up.

Why do people say too much?

There is a great tendency for people to say more than they should or need to. They usually do this for some very positive reasons!

- They are keen to demonstrate how much they know about the subject.
- They want to be helpful.
- They want to demonstrate that they have done their homework, or
- They just love their subject!

Unfortunately, these tendencies, whilst reflecting positive features, can have negative consequences. Flooding the audience with information can detract from the message. Enthusiasm needs to be balanced by conciseness.

Even though people tend to want to talk for a long time, experience suggests that the best presentations usually last *no longer than about 20 minutes*. If required to go on for longer it is best to break the presentation up a bit or to make it very interactive. For example, a 40 minute presentation could be broken into two segments with questions at the end of each segment.

The information iceberg

The best way of illustrating how to organise the information you have on a particular topic is by reference to a diagram we call the "Information Iceberg".

The iceberg represents the total knowledge you might have on a particular topic. The object of the brainstorming exercise is to identify the most important information for the particular audience you are presenting to. How much information is required will be determined by the amount of time you have

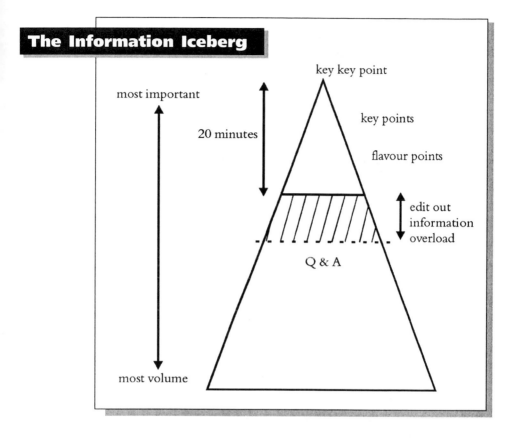

The Information Iceberg

available for the presentation. The temptation is to draw the line too low. This results in you, the presenter, trying to pack too much information into too little time. You end up either having to speak faster, in order to get the content across in the allotted time, or delivering at a sensible pace and over-running your allotted time.

Limiting the number of key points is often very difficult to achieve in practice. Here is one technique you may find helpful. Deliberately highlight a number of aspects about your subject and then state that most will be ignored in your presentation!

Below you will see an example of a word-slide covering health and safety issues. The presenter made the mistake of covering all ten items.

Example   **Health & safety**

1. Assessment of the workplace.

2. Identification of hazards which affect health.

3. Application of standards of control.

4. Identification of socio-economic, political and cultural factors which affect health at work.

5. Epidemiology and research.

6. Risk avoidance.

7. Educational needs of the workforce.

8. Promotion of critical awareness.

9. Health promotion.

10. Understanding physiological and psychological aspects of ill health.

The audience remembered little of what was said. The presenter would have fared much better if he had:

● Begun the presentation strongly - perhaps relating a short story about some safety issue to engage the audience's attention.

● Shown the slide and then said that he would concentrate on just two key issues, such as risk avoidance and a health promotion day.

By using this approach the audience would have seen that the presenter hadn't forgotten any important aspects and, indeed, was prepared to answer questions on them. They would have appreciated that he or she was focusing on relevant key issues as well as the subliminal message - which may have been to persuade listeners to take the subject more seriously.

Structure

Having decided what you want to say, the next step is to structure this content in such a way that you persuade your audience to listen to every word. This ideal is seldom achieved. In reality, listeners follow a predictable pattern. Initially, they will listen with full attention and, if intrigued, will listen further. However, if you fail to catch their attention they will drift away. If this happens, they will not start to listen intently again until towards the end as the speaker sums up. Two key points arise out of this:

● First, the conventional wisdom of "Tell'em what you going to tell'em, tell'em, and then tell'em what you told'em" is somewhat suspect!

● Second, you have to say something that will attract the audience right from the very start. Avoid conventional openings that follow a predictable track.

Practical points

Make a strong start

Our advice is to make a start strong. Say something that will attract the audience. Don't feel you have to thank your audience or go through other conventions at the start.

Case study
My firm once helped a senior banker with a major conference speech about helping firms do business in the EC. He had far too many points to cover and a very dull opening pitch. We managed to find a provocative fact buried deep in the script which we pulled out and used to replace the soporific start.

"Last year the French received 25% of the European Regional Development Grant. Guess what the British received? The answer is 3%. Why so little? The answer is we don't know how to use the system ..."

This approach uses a stark fact to act as bait. The audience feel compelled to want to hear more. Some are even stirred and upset that the French have done so much better than the British.

Another approach is to focus the audience on the key issue.

Case study

An aviation engineer was talking about aircraft structure.

"If you hold a Coke can in your hands you know it's not very strong. You can squeeze and crush it. What you may not know is that the skin of our aircraft is only four times the thickness of that Coke can.

If your car hits a pothole at 20 mph you would expect the suspension to survive. Likewise, we need to have undercarriages strong enough to allow a plane to land at 130 knots in a strong crosswind. But if you drive your car over a 100 foot cliff both you and the car will be written off. You're dead!

Cars cannot be designed for that event and, in the same way, we cannot design aircraft to remain intact in all situations.

I want to talk to you today about the design principles we apply when making a plane. In particular, making it strong but not too strong to complete its primary task."

This approach illustrates a different kind of strong start. It appeals to non technical people who immediately understand a fundamental point. Interestingly, other experts in the audience will like it too. Their reaction might be "That's an interesting way to put it" or even "The old fool got that one right". The point is that by starting in an anecdotal way, relating a complex subject to an everyday example which could be recognised by everyone in the audience, the speaker was able to make what he was saying understandable and fascinating.

Avoid abstraction

From what we discussed earlier you have established why you are speaking, your key points and a structure of sorts. Many presenters fail at this stage because the subject they are trying to put across to the audience, while food and drink to them, is essentially abstract to the audience. *Abstraction is a major reason why messages fail to strike home.*

We can illustrate abstraction by discussing Daisy, who is a cow. This is quite specific and even a small child looking over a fence can quickly grasp the concept of a single cow called Daisy. But when that child sees other cows she may well say "Look Mummy, more Daisies". She might be corrected and told they are cows. A stage further up the ladder would be to describe all animals on this farm as livestock. The farm also has cereal crops so the term "mixed farm" could be used. Finally, we could describe the whole farm as a "wealth creation unit".

Wealth creation unit
Mixed farm
Livestock
Cows
Daisy

The point we are making here is that words like "wealth", "quality", "empowered" and "management" fit onto the top rung of our "Ladder of Abstraction". You may have to use such words, but confusion or misunderstanding will occur if you don't come down the ladder to give a more vivid picture of what you are driving at.

Make key points come alive

So how do you make key points stand out and come alive? And how do you ensure these points are talked about later? We suggest there are two broad approaches:

● Use visual aids.
● Use creative ideas such as those used by radio journalists to conjure up a picture and avoid abstraction.

Most presenters will opt for using visual aids to help make the subject more understandable and memorable. We believe visuals can be helpful, and sometimes essential, to communicate certain types of information. However, the brain also likes the mental images that we can conjure up from our imagination. Here we plunder the radio journalist's tool box and steal his ideas. These are:

● Analogy.
● Vivid example.
● Story/case study.

Analogy

As was illustrated in the Coke can example, analogies can be very effective. However, they are difficult to create from scratch. There is no software programme devoted to analogy. You are on your own! Actually it's not that bad. It may well be you have someone in your team who has a talent for dreaming them up. Perhaps you have heard an analogy that is a bit risqué but you could clean it up. In short, be on the prowl for good analogies. Steal them. Adapt them. Above all realise that a well placed analogy is more likely to be remembered than a picture slide. Did the engineer have to show a picture of the Coke can?

Vivid example

Examples are more straightforward than analogies. However, you must be careful that the examples are not too abstract in themselves. The examples must be vivid.

Case study   I once listened to a talk on the impact of Information Technology on the running of supermarkets. It was dull and abstract, although the speaker evidently thought it important. His examples were impossible to visualise. After some prodding he came back with an example involving bananas.

"We need to get bananas from the warehouse to the supermarket at precisely the right moment. Housewives won't buy bananas which are flecked with black spots nor will they buy green ones. What they want is yellow bananas with some green in the stem. Our new IT system with bar coding allows us to monitor the flow of bananas from warehouse to shop floor at the right moment to avoid waste and appeal to our customer, the housewife."

This approach is at the "Daisy the Cow" level. The example is vivid and avoids using too much technical jargon. The point is made. The point will be remembered.

Story/case study

We are all conditioned from early childhood to being told stories. Our brains can create a structure based on the story so find it easier to remember the points of detail. Even the most boring, technical subject can be transformed with this tool.

We recently helped a top law firm promote information about employment law. The detail was intense and difficult to follow so we concocted a tongue-in-cheek story.

Imagine the scene. You return to your office to find in your in-tray an urgent memo to discuss the problem of Miss Overcoat. She has been with the firm for 18 months and is a disaster. Late for work, constantly on the phone to organise her social life, she has failed to meet any of her performance targets. She has been warned both face to face and in writing. As she has been with the firm for less than two years (and therefore has reduced employment protection rights) it should be a relatively straightforward matter to dismiss her.

Then you remember that there was an article in the papers about a case of unfair dismissal going to the House of Lords. The case concerned another woman (who had also been with a company for less than two years), who had successfully argued that women are discriminated against and thus the two-year limit was too long. The limit might now be reduced to one year.

Later another character was introduced who also had employment problems. The point here is that by introducing cartoon-like characters, almost like in a comic strip, you help to keep people focused on the main issue whilst being able to explore the detail. Again, we are back to Daisy the cow, but in a different form.

Use mini-summaries

Most people would agree that it is sensible to summarise at the end of a presentation. We would also advise you to summarise at certain points *during* the presentation, most particularly after you have developed a key theme and wish to go on to the next one.

The point here is that, no matter how well you deliver a presentation, people's attention can still drift. By using regular mini-summaries, you can bring your audience back into the fold, giving them the chance to get back into focus and listen to the rest of your talk. Failure to summarise, on the other hand, can cause listeners effectively to tune out for long periods and then feel embarrassed. So much so that they might feel inhibited at asking you questions in case they betray the fact that they had dropped off somewhere along the line.

Make a strong ending

It would seem logical enough to end a presentation with a summary to draw together the key themes of your talk. It is very helpful if, as you do so, you refer to some of the vivid examples you may have used earlier.

If your aim is to persuade or inspire then your personal conviction needs to come through at this stage. This is where you want to get your personality across. Don't rely on a list of words up on the screen, speak directly to your audience. "I cannot hide from you the fact that we will face many difficult challenges in the immediate future as we start to produce a 600 seater aircraft. But I also know we've faced similar challenges in the past. I know we have a superb team – all of you here. In a few years time you will look back and say we got it right. We made the hard decisions. We made the right decisions."

Presentations often end on a note of hype and abstraction, for example, "We must provide a standard of customer satisfaction better than the customer expects". This type of statement sounds worthy enough but really doesn't make much impact. It is too vague. It is much better to link such statements to a tangible example given earlier in the talk. Often the speaker describes a graphic example of exceptional customer service but at the end merely refers to it in a vague, abstract way. Be specific, link in the example, eg "Like the chemist (about whom the speaker had spoken earlier) we have got to provide a standard of service better than the customer expects".

The use of language

No chapter on content is complete without a look at the use of words and language.

Here we introduce the concept of "Language Hierarchy", which is not to be confused with the Ladder of Abstraction.

Language hierarchy

We can identify five primary levels of language:

Formal
Semi-formal
Normal
Colloquial
Slang

Taking the word "car" as normal idiom we would accept "motor" as colloquial and "wheels" as slang. Going in the opposite direction, we would consider "automobile" as semi-formal and "ground transportation system" as formal. Try this same exercise with "policeman".

Our ears are used to listening to language from within a lower circle of the bottom three levels whereas our eyes are used to language from within an upper circle.

Take this a step further and we quickly spot that simple, single syllable words tend to be more powerful and effective than their multi-syllabled sisters. "Stop", "start", "go", "get" and "but" have more oomph than "terminate", "initiate", "proceed", "obtain" and "however". Most of these simple, single syllable words are of Anglo Saxon, rather than Latin, origin. Here are some more:

Permit = let
Obtain = buy
Wealthy = rich
Violate = break
Hearing impaired = deaf

One of the hallmarks of a good speaker is their ability to use good, lower circle language and avoid stuffy and long-winded upper circle prose.

Jargon

On a similar note, speakers should use terms and phrases everyone can understand. Most businesses and professions have their own language, their own jargon. People who work in those professions use the language amongst themselves. But problems arise when they try to communicate to people outside their professional sphere.

An effective presenter will purge his language of any technical terms and industry jargon except when dealing with colleagues and peers. No one is ever offended by Plain English.

People outside a profession generally know far less about the technicalities of the profession than an expert would ever imagine. The expert, who is immersed in the minutiae and jargon of his profession, cannot conceive how little outsiders know about his subject. If the presenter starts with the premise that his audience know virtually nothing, he will be less likely to fog his argument in technical language. This does not mean that the argument should be simple-minded but only that the language should be clear. As someone once said, "eschew obfuscation" (avoid bewilderment).

Preparation process for a conference

You have accepted an invitation to speak at a conference. Before looking in detail at how to decide what your message is and how to structure it for maximum effect, you should consider the whole presentation process (and what it involves) from the moment you have a date in the diary to the delivery of the presentation. In skeleton form, the process looks like this.

EVENT

↓

PREPARATION PHASE

CHECKING

REHEARSAL

DELIVERY

Q & A SESSION

The event

Find out as much about the event as you can. There are many questions you will need answered before you can start preparing and structuring what you are going to say. Ask yourself:

- Who is organising the event?
- Is it really appropriate for me to participate in this event?
- Who are the audience?

  - how many people will there be?
  - what are their expectations?
  - what is their level of knowledge?
  - what misconceptions will I have to correct?
  - are there any prejudices I should anticipate?

- What is the theme of the event?
- What shall I call my subject?
- Where is the event taking place?

  - will I be speaking from a lectern or podium?
  - will I have lighting and a microphone?
  - what seating arrangements are there?

- When does the event start?

  - what time is my presentation?
  - how long would my presentation be?

- Am I the only speaker in my part of the programme?
  - will I be introduced by the organiser? If not, by whom?
  - who else will speak?
  - what will they be speaking about?
- Will there be a discussion or Q & A session after my presentation?

Preparation phase

This phase can be broken down into four distinct parts:

- Brainstorming.
- Research.
- Structure.
- Visual aids.

Checking

If you are presenting to an external audience, you might need to run your presentation past those in your organisation who have either a financial, legal or public relations interest in what you plan to say.

Rehearsal

Once you have completed putting the presentation together you need to rehearse it. This includes coordinating visual aids which may have been prepared separately.

Delivery

Deliver your presentation using either a script, notes or ad–lib.

Q & A session

Not every presentation has a Q & A session but for those that do this is a critical phase. If not prepared for properly, all the good work achieved in the formal part of your presentation can be undone.

Conclusion

For a conference where you are leading a number of speakers the above process becomes more complex, although the principles are the same.

The main problem we encounter is individuals who wait until the last minute to prepare and produce scripts that are far too long.

I know of one company that insists on initial scripts and draft slides being discussed at a coordination meeting a clear month before the event. They also insist on a proper dress rehearsal 24 hours before the event with a visual aids expert in close support.

Chapter 5 – contents

Visual aids

Do you agree or disagree with these statements?

S1. The listener receives more information through his eyes than his ears.

S2. When showing a list of words, I uncover them one by one to avoid the audience reading ahead.

S3. I use word-slides to remind me where I am and to give the audience a chance to keep up with me.

S4. You should use the best available computer-generated slides to give the impression of being at the cutting edge.

S5. Software packages like PowerPoint, CorelDraw and Freelance are great. They save a lot of time in preparation.

S6. I like to have a continuous visual display throughout the presentation as it helps to keep the audience's interest and stops them switching off.

See page 70 for our comments.

Introduction

This chapter considers visual aids and their use. Looking first at both strategic and stage management issues, the chapter concludes with a review of computer-generated visual aids.

Strategic issues

Our starting point is to ask two simple questions.

● Does the use of visual aids improve the clarity and memorability of the message?
● Does the use of visual aids get in the way of the personality? (We have to be negative about this point as visual aids are unlikely to do much to *enhance* the strength or persuasion of the personality.)

If you are busy and don't wish to browse or look at minor detail then go straight to "**Key issues**". It is particularly important that senior managers buy into these key issues. Even if they don't have much opportunity to use visuals themselves, they are likely to be in a position to influence their subordinates.

Too many presenters are influenced by company culture or what they perceive to be the norm. They deluge their audience with vast amounts of dull or over-busy visuals. This practice has been increased by the introduction of computer-generated visuals.

We believe that visual aids are often the best way of displaying complex information, and that computer-generated visuals can add particular advantages. However, we encourage people to think carefully about using these aids, and to make sure that they earn their place in a formal presentation, and are not used as a substitute for creative ideas. They should not obscure the personality of the presenter (who is, after all, the most important visual aid!), especially if the presenter wishes to influence their audience.

We live in a highly visual age. Years ago there wasn't much beyond the blackboard. Then, in the Sixties, a magic machine called the Overhead Projector (OHP) came onto the scene. We were taught to use the "beast" with much uncovering of acetates and manipulation of flips that were overlaid at the crucial moment. At the same time 35mm transparencies became more widely used.

Since then we have rocketed ahead with flip-charts, whiteboards, videos, electronic boards and a vast array of computer-generated visuals.

Recent advances in systems mean that laptops now have the power to handle multimedia packages which show reasonable quality pictures, including video and film clips with sound.

These are exciting developments, and inevitably expectations rise. However, there is concern that the cumulative effect of these new technologies will be to shorten people's attention span. We now have a deluge of visual information. The Victorians were used to sitting for considerable lengths of time and paying attention. Nowadays, many of us work long hours under pressure. We have a lot more paper to read. We watch TV and computer screens. We use our eyes more than our ears.

Hands up those of you who can remember dealing with Roneo machines or correcting a foolscap skin with bright red special ink? Can you remember life before the photocopier? How many of you listen to a radio play or journalistic report rather than watch TV?

Why use visuals anyway?

This may sound like a ridiculous question, but it bears consideration. We always ask our delegates why they use visuals. Here are some of their answers:

- I am expected to. It's the way we always do it in our company.
- They make me look well prepared.
- They remind me what to say next.
- It's simpler to pick up some slides and put them up than start from scratch.
- My audience expect me to. If I didn't use them people would think I had been idle.

- It looks high tech and state-of-the-art-to use PowerPoint and the like so I hope to impress my listeners.
- My audience need to be entertained, after all my subject is pretty tedious.

All these reasons have some logic, but they miss an important truth. A visual aid may be able to show information more effectively than words alone. A map of South America, a picture of a new product or a graph showing market trends are adding value to what the presenter is saying – no doubt you would agree. But what about showing visuals that don't really add much value? Does it matter?

This is a difficult issue and one that often produces strong debate. However, in our opinion, using such visuals can have negative effects. The key issues are outlined below.

Key issues

Saturation

The problem

Our eyes are able to absorb information much faster than our ears. For example, we can listen to someone talking at 120 words a minute but we can read at about 300 words a minute. This suggests that visuals are good news. But wait a minute. The same brain has to process all this information. If we present slide after slide of complex information then most listeners will start to turn off. They haven't actually fallen asleep but they may as well have done as they are not processing any information. It may well be that the fifth pie-chart of your presentation was the most crucial, but some listeners may have turned off ages ago. Many presenters fall into this trap.

People vary. We all have widely different attention spans. A controlled, analytical person will stay focused longer than someone who continually seeks to be stimulated and wants to know the bottom line, but not the grinding detail, of how to get there. Some of us find visually displayed information easier to absorb, others prefer the spoken word.

The solution

Below we list a number of possible solutions. Of course, these are not panaceas and you should always take into account your individual circumstances before applying them.

- Cut back on the number of slides you use. Make each one earn its place, ask yourself, "Does this slide add to what I am saying?" Don't be afraid not to use any visuals at all.
- Top and tail. In other words, begin the presentation with no visuals at all. You, the presenter, command the audience's attention. Again, at the end, drop the visuals. Switch off the projector. Now address your audience, putting your personal spin on what you want the audience to take away.
- Be prepared to use blank slides. Use either black, which makes it appear that the projector has been turned off, or a light pastel colour and small logo. This forces the audience to focus on you.
- Keep slides simple. It's obvious advice but do be rigorous in cutting out unnecessary detail. If you can't; tell the audience to ignore certain aspects and point to the relevant parts. Better still, build up the information bit by bit.
- Remember the alternatives to visuals – vivid spoken examples, anecdotes and analogies are often much more effective.

Competition

The problem

Up goes the slide and straightaway you, the presenter, launch into an explanation. Sounds reasonable, and it is often done. But if the slide is complex the audience face a dilemma. Do they listen to you first or orientate themselves to the picture? If it's a graph most people agree that the first thing the brain does is to respond to the visual by checking out the X & Y axis. It then tries to work out what is going on in the middle. In the meantime, you are droning on in the background. If the slide is simple then there really isn't a problem, but for complex images that are new to the audience you need to do something different.

The solution

Example | **No slide up at all.** "Let me tell you about how much inflation has come down in Latin America. Fifteen years ago some countries had inflation rates of 1000% a month. Now the majority have settled down to around 15% a year. I'll show you this slide that explains what has happened in three countries – Argentina, Uruguay and Brazil." **The slide now goes up, followed by silence. You then add any extra comments or information.** "Of course I only showed three countries but the story is about the same for most others."

We call this technique "Priming the Pump".

We try to get an audience to form an image in their minds first and then physically show it to them. They will lock on to the image far more quickly that way.

Remember, with complex slides you need to give the audience time to tune in.

- Prime the pump.
- Don't read out information (unless you want to give special emphasis) – the audience can read perfectly well for themselves.
- Don't face towards the visual except when you want your audience to look at it. The act of you turning towards it sends an obvious signal.

Over-use of word-slides

The problem

Many presenters use word-slides as a backdrop prompt to remind them what to say. They believe it helps the audience to keep on track.

This approach has a flaw. If you put up a list of ten points and concentrate on point one, how can you be sure your audience aren't scanning down the list and wondering what you are going to say about point four? In other words, are you giving the audience a reason not to listen to you?

Of course, a list which acts as an agenda or a summary is clearly helpful. Similarly, displaying a list of words as a route map can be helpful, allowing the presenter to lead the audience from one point to the next. Word-slides outlining the key points of a speech or presentation can also be of benefit when presenting to an audience whose English is weak.

However, beware of using too many word-slides, you will bore your audience rigid! Initially word-slides do no harm, but eventually they act in a negative way as yet another "laundry list" is displayed. When questioned after such a presentation most people agree they can never remember what was on the word-slides.

The solution

- Use word-slides only when you think they earn their place.
- Don't bother with the uncover technique unless you have a strong reason. PowerPoint and other packages are an exception as you can make words "fly in" under control.
- Use creative ideas that are memorable and stimulating.

Over-complex visuals

The problem

The next point is so obvious I can almost hear you yawn. However, it must be made. Over-complex visuals do not strike home, they leave the listener feeling inadequate. They can also be very difficult to decipher from the back of a room.

Other, less obvious, problems with complex slides are that the presenter is tempted to say too much in an attempt to be helpful or tries to display an intergalactic knowledge of the subject under discussion!

The solution

- Keep things simple. No more words than can fit onto a T-shirt.
- Be prepared to build up complex ideas in simple steps.
- Be disciplined about what you say. Use notes to remind you when to stop.

Quick summary

Many people, for all sorts of reasons, don't use visual aids properly. Usually they overdo it. The original objectives of presenting - that both the presenter's message and personality are successfully projected to the audience - get lost in a mass of detail.

We encourage people to:

- Use visuals when they earn their place.
- Avoid competing with their own visual aid.
- Avoid endless lists of word-slides.
- Avoid complexity, except where it is absolutely necessary.

Visual aids should be our servant, not our master. If we wish to persuade, influence, inspire, lead and encourage other people then it's the clarity of our ideas and our sense of conviction that will win the day.

Case study I was sitting in The Queen Elizabeth II Hall in London a few years ago to listen to a major presentation on the state of the aviation industry by a well-known aircraft finance leasing company. They had gone to considerable trouble. A production company had been used to arrange the stage set and create superb quality colour slides. The audience were from the financial community who had the money to invest, if persuaded.

The President of the leasing company stood up to speak and the lights went down. The slide show began. The first few slides were fine – clear pie-charts showing proportions of sales in different sectors around the world. However, after about fifteen slides I found myself mentally loaded up with as much information as I really wanted. I didn't fall asleep but watched the reaction of others. At the outset most of them were leaning forward in their seats jotting down the odd note, however, as time went by, pens were put down and most people slumped back in their seats.

We were suffering from an excess of information. We were still listening in a glazed sort of way but no longer processing the ideas. After 40 minutes of continuous visual information the presenters staggered to a halt. We had just three questions and then left clutching large packs with copies of all the slides. In the drinks session afterwards I spoke to some of the audience.

They were impressed by the show but, when pushed, had to admit they couldn't remember the key messages. As for the personalities, they had no impact whatsoever except during the rather embarrassingly short Q & A session. The next day the *Financial Times* gave a rather critical report of the occasion. This is a typical situation that in greater or lesser forms is being repeated throughout the business world.

Stage management issues

So far all our advice has been directed towards ensuring that visual aids help with the clarity of the message and don't get in the way of the presenter's personality. Now we offer both general (basic) and specific advice on stage management issues.

The basics

First, make sure everyone will be able to see any visual. Walk around the room and crouch down to seat level. With large audiences the screen has to be raised up.

The most difficult rooms are those that are long and thin. You may have to move the audience through 90 degrees so that they are then in a short fat room!

Also, make sure that everyone will be able to hear you. A microphone might seem unnecessary in rehearsal but a large audience absorb sound like a blanket.

Second, check heating and cooling systems and levels of noise. It always gets hotter once a large group gathers. Not every venue has good air-conditioning, yet to leave the windows open may attract unwelcome noise.

Finally, check any equipment beforehand to see that it works. Murphy is always on the prowl! (Murphy's law states that if something can go wrong, it will!) In particular, you should check that there is:

● Enough extension cable.
● Enough plug sockets in the right place.
● Suitable lighting in the room. Can it be turned down? If it can, is there a lectern light for the speaker? In a large room the speaker needs some sort of horizontal spot light. Otherwise, the lectern light will shine up their nose and make them look like Count Dracula!

The specifics

Litepro/Epson/Sony multimedia systems

Practical points

- Make sure you know how any multimedia system works. Again, check remote controls and lighting levels.
- Have an escape plan if all else fails. For example, with PowerPoint you should make A4 hard copies of your slides.

Video

Video is likely to be used increasingly as the range of multimedia projectors and camcorders on the market expands.

Practical points

- Video with sound is a powerful medium so use it in short bursts otherwise it will steal the show or make all other devices seem lack lustre.
- Use it on long presentations as entertainment and to provide an opportunity for the audience to relax.
- Use it to provide third party credibility. A short clip of your customer extolling your virtues has an authentic ring to it. This used to require expert help but nowadays many people understand the basics of operating a camcorder.

Overhead projectors

Overhead projectors are versatile and good in most situations. However, there can be problems.

A typical problem with OHP's is that they can act as a barrier, obscuring the audience's view of the presenter. You can sometimes lower the projector by putting it on a chair and then cranking the reflector mirror up. Another solution is to offset the projector so that it is not an obstacle and angle the screen so that the picture can be seen without distortion.

Practical points

- Find the on/off switch – it's not always obvious!
- Bring a spare bulb - vital.
- Avoid projector glare. Put masking tape along the edges of slides so that light doesn't glare out at the edges.
- Stand by the screen rather than next to the projector. This means people can focus on the presenter and the visual at the same time.

35mm projectors

35mm projectors produce good quality pictures, the slides are compact and travel well. However, bear in mind that the lights have to be turned down when using these projectors, which can make the audience feel disconnected and even sleepy!

Practical points

- Do you have a remote control, or do you trust someone else to move the slides along?
- Can you control the lighting in the room?
- What can you do if the projector jams?

Flip-charts

Flip-charts are versatile, easy to use and highly reliable. They are fine for small groups but no good for groups of 50 or more.

Practical points

- Use thick felt-tip pens and large writing.
- Sketch out some pencil grid boxes on the charts to help you get the right size and spacing for your wording or figures.
- Use black, blue and red pens as they stand out well. Avoid yellow, magenta and green, which can be difficult to see.
- Leave blank sheets between items as writing can show through.

Charts and graphs

Charts and graphs have a very useful (and sometimes essential) role in displaying numerical data and organisational structure.

Below are some comments on the main types.

Straight graphs - These are good for showing trends over a period of time but you can distort the figures if you aren't careful, or perhaps you meant to anyway! For example, having the X & Y axis starting at a value other than zero.

Pie-charts - These are great for showing proportions or relative size.

Flow-charts - These are good for simplifying complicated procedures.

Organisational charts - I always find these surprisingly useful in establishing who reports to whom. They are particularly valuable when describing matrix organisations, which can be very complicated.

Bar-charts - These are a good alternative to straight graphs and can be used to show different kinds of data.

Tables - These tend to be boring and rather busy. I encourage people to leave out some of the detail. Not every line has to be shown.

Handouts

Handouts are given out to audiences to take away and read later. In reality, however, they rarely get read.

Practical points
● We advise against giving handouts at the start of a presentation. They will draw attention away from you, the presenter. Of course, this is not always possible. City analysts, for example, insist on handouts in advance.

● Handouts should be capable of being understood later. A list of bullet points may not mean much a week later. We are great believers in one page summaries. Well written they are read, and remembered.

Music

On large occasions music can help create an atmosphere. A disco beat will get people more excited. Something calmer will create a more contemplative mood. For something festive or jolly a stirring military band might be the thing. Clearly, the type of music you use will be influenced by the nature of the subject, the presenters and the audience. Typically, a sales team like being jazzed up - and almost expect it.

Short skits and plays

There is sometimes an opportunity to be more creative by laying a small skit or play. For example, the presenter can start making statements that are plainly wrong. The audience become concerned but then a stooge challenges the speaker and they go into a rehearsed act. It's great fun and highly effective. The trick is to keep it simple.

Computer-generated visual aids

Like it or not, computer-generated visual aids have arrived! PowerPoint, being a Microsoft product, is probably the best known package that produces them, but others, such as Harvard Graphics, Freelance and CorelDraw, are also in common use. On the whole, the general principles don't change much so I will refer to PowerPoint for simplicity.

It is helpful to look at PowerPoint and its colleagues in two ways.

First, they can be used to construct graphics, charts, words and clip art. They can also store images, pictures and sound.

Second, whatever is created on computer can then be:

- Printed out on A4 paper through a printer.
- Printed onto acetates for an OHP through a printer (whether laser or inkjet, but inkjets are much cheaper for colour printing at present).
- Projected onto a screen via a tablet on top of an OHP. (In other words, a flat screen like that on a laptop but which looks like a small window frame. A powerful 1000 watt bulb from the OHP punches through the window displaying the information).
- Projected by machines that look like mis-shapen 35mm projectors but which are in fact sophisticated multimedia systems that can be remotely controlled and show slides, films and sound. Typical names are Litepro, Epson and Sony. These systems are expensive, at around £2,000 upwards, but prices are falling and quality is going up. It's important to get one with the right amount of lumens. In a large room, holding a hundred people or more, you will need a machine with more than 200 lumens. At a recent conference I used a 1000 lumen model.

So why are we all going for the new world of computer-generated visual aids?

Advantages

- They are cheap to produce. Leaving aside projection systems, we can save a lot of money. Producing 35mm slides is expensive whereas software expense is tiny.
- They offer tremendous flexibility. We can change information at the last minute – something we can't do with slides. Indeed, we can change spreadsheet type information on the spot in response to a question. We can also change the order of slides in an instant, moving from slide 5 to 13 in a flash.
- They look good. True, we can generate professional looking slides. However, although the overall quality may be good,

photographs tend to look a bit fuzzy unless you are using the very best projection system. Recently I heard that Saatchis were invited to "downgrade" their pictures to allow them to be compatible with the projector. Old fashioned 35mm colour slides would have been better in this case!

● The hardware is portable. For many presenters this means carrying a laptop. A whole presentation can be on a floppy disc or CD-ROM, although you must be confident that there is a reliable projection system at the far end.

Disadvantages

● Our comments about saturation and competition are particulary relevant to the use of these visuals. Some software packages actively encourage us to build ever more complex slide shows! Beware, it's seductive stuff.

● There is a trend towards standardisation. Presentations are starting to look the same. Many use the same template background, usually a picture of the world. In competitive pitches it's going to be even harder to differentiate your product or service if you and your competitor have given what appear to be identical presentations.

● Although aspects of PowerPoint and other packages can save time, there is quite a steep learning curve if you are going to do more than produce some word-slides. It may be best to send someone from your administrative staff on an appropriate course. Senior executives should not be spending their time constructing intricate charts!

Summary

● Cut back on the number of slides you use. Make each one earn its place. Don't be afraid not to use any visuals.

● Top and tail. In other words, begin the presentation with no visuals at all. You, the presenter, command the audience's attention. Again, at the end, drop the visuals. Switch off the projector. Now address your audience, putting your personal spin on what you want the audience to take away.

- Be prepared to use blank slides. With PowerPoint this can be done by pressing "B" on the keyboard or having a series of blank slides available at short notice to be moved into place.

- Keep slides simple. It's obvious advice but do be rigorous in cutting out unnecessary detail. If you can't, then tell the audience to ignore certain aspects and point to the relevant parts. Better still, build up the information bit by bit.

- Remember the alternatives – vivid spoken examples, anecdotes and analogies are often much more effective.

- With complex slides give the audience time to orientate themselves first.

- Prime the pump.

- Don't read out information the audience can read perfectly well for themselves, unless you want to give special emphasis.

- Let words "fly in" under control.

- Avoid the obvious temptation of preparing a presentation by pulling out a selection of visuals from your "library" and using them to form a structure. It is very tempting to do this, especially when you are busy. However, you should always plan a presentation by establishing your key points and general structure *first* without referring to any visuals at all. Having established your structure you can then start to consider what visuals might bring greater clarity to your presentation.

- Avoid well-known clip art images or standard templates. The effect is lost.

- Make sure your projection system is strong enough for everyone to see. A gloomy tablet is much worse than a bright but old fashioned OHP or clear flip-chart.

- Make sure all the technical bits work and have a back up.

Quiz answers

A1. Agree. It's true, the eye is a more powerful sensor than the ear. It can read words four times quicker than the ear can hear the same words when spoken. The ear, however, can pick up on nuances and emphases. Can you imagine Churchill's speeches put up on a series of visual aids?

A2. Disagree. Don't bother with this technique unless you have a particular reason. Most audiences find it annoying.

A3. Disagree. It sounds logical enough but over-use of word-slides can be boring and distracting in practice. They can, however, be helpful to those whose understanding of English is patchy.

A4. Perhaps. Computer-generated slides, properly projected, are impressive, but don't forget the human element. If your objective is to build trust and develop a relationship then a glitzy slide show may defeat that.

A5. Perhaps. PowerPoint and other software packages can save lots of time but I have seen senior executives wasting valuable energy engrossed in the minutiae of constructing a pie-chart.

A6. Disagree. In most cases your objective as presenter is to persuade, influence or encourage and therefore your personality has got to come across positively to the audience. A continuous visual display will relegate your personality to a voice over.

Chapter 6 – contents

Question and answer sessions

Do you agree or disagree with the following statements?

S1. Some people are naturally good on their feet but I should try to avoid question and answer (Q & A) sessions as it is not my scene.

S2. I believe that long, detailed answers help to satisfy the questioner.

S3. I enjoy the cut and thrust of questions but sometimes wonder if I get carried away and say too much.

S4. I take handling questions seriously and try to anticipate the worst questions I might face.

See page 82 for our comments.

Introduction

Some people make dreadful presentations but then come to life during the Q & A session. They seem to regain their enthusiasm and passion for the subject. But there are also many people who present well but then blow it when answering questions. This can be for a number of reasons.

Some presenters feel ill at ease with questions because they are not on top of the subject they are talking about. More frequently, however, the presenter over-estimates the audience's level of knowledge. You are probably much more of an expert in your field than you think, especially after all the preparation work you have done!

Listeners ask questions for a number of reasons:

● To seek clarification or expansion of your subject.
● To probe the strength of your argument.
● To impress others in the audience, perhaps their boss.
● To make a statement or influence others.
● To use the occasion to fly some kite of their own.

You, on the other hand, may also use the session as an opportunity to "sell" some key point which you felt should not come out in the main presentation. It gives you the opportunity to demonstrate the depth of your knowledge. It also gives you another chance to sell your idea, yourself or other members of your team.

Our advice covers:

● The basics.
● Handling difficult questions.
● Stage management issues.

The basics

Practical points

Pause

Before answering any question, pause. By pausing you may do yourself a favour for three reasons:

- First, you are more likely to hear the whole question and come out with a well structured answer.
- Second, you pay a compliment to the questioner. They see you having to think, which shows you take their question seriously. When Sir Robin Day was asked what question he would most liked to have asked the then Prime Minister, Margaret Thatcher, he replied, "Prime Minister, what is the answer to my next question?" He found her habit of answering before he had even finished posing a question extremely irritating.
- Third, just like a poker player, by consistently pausing in a hostile situation you tend to "hide your hand". The questioner finds you more difficult to read. You also look confident and relaxed.

If the question is unclear

If the question is unclear, don't hesitate to ask for clarification because, if you guess at the meaning of a question, you may end up confusing everybody! Rather than a blunt "I don't understand" you could restate the question on your own terms. "What I think you are saying is …" or "What lies behind your question is …" You could then ask the questioner whether your interpretation is correct. This is not an aggressive technique and if you did get the meaning of the question wrong then the onus is on the questioner to correct you.

Repeat the question

With a large audience consider repeating the question or rephrasing it. Remember, not everyone may be able to hear the question, particularly if it comes from the front of the audience.

Avoid over-answering

"I only asked you the time and you told me how to build a watch."

Many presenters over-answer. We recommend you keep answers short! Long answers are dangerous as they can:

- Turn people off and, once bored, an audience will stop asking questions.
- Leave the listener even more confused than before the question was asked.
- Cause you to say more than you meant to and reveal sensitive or confidential information.

Case study I recently attended a major conference on airline leasing finance. The speakers hadn't presented well because they had swamped us with far too much information and had displayed an unrelenting list of complex slides. We were delighted when it came to question time.

The first question was put and the chairman began to answer at length but then asked his colleagues on the stage to add their pennyworth as well. Eventually question two was asked. After three questions there were no more. By their long and ponderous answers the speakers had caused the audience to hesitate to ask any more.

Use a notepad

You are often faced with a multiple or complex question. A few hasty notes will help to keep you on track. Taking time to jot down some points also shows the listener that you are taking the question seriously.

End the Q & A session strongly

Try to end the Q & A session on a strong note rather than allowing things to peter out. Wait until you have given a brilliant answer! If this doesn't happen then throw in your own question, which you then answer yourself.

Ask questions

Many presenters don't realise that they can ask questions too! This can be a very powerful tool and it is a useful way of breaking up the one-way communication flow of one party always asking the questions and one party answering.

When speakers are in presenting mode they don't always find it easy to switch over to asking questions themselves.

By taking time to find out more about the questioner or the nature of the question, you will give a more effective answer. Asking questions will also, of course, draw a response from the questioner and this can help the questioner to convince themselves rather than having to be convinced by the presenter. For example, a questioner could ask the presenter how his proposed method would work in the day-to-day operation of running a company. Instead of answering this question directly the presenter could say, "Well John, let us see how this could work in your particular situation. How would you implement my ideas?" Remember, people are much more likely to be convinced by their own arguments and responses than by you as a presenter, who they believe will want to "sell" them something.

Handling difficult questions

Practical points

Plan ahead

We can all expect to face difficult questions at some time but how often do we plan a strategy to tackle them? When we are preparing a presentation we should always try to spot what the tough and difficult questions might be. Better still, rehearse these difficult questions beforehand with colleagues.

If you don't know the answer

If you don't know the answer to a question, you have three choices:

- Admit the fact straightaway and, if appropriate, make a commitment to find out.
- Seek answers from other people in the audience.
- Refer the questioner to another person or an alternative source of information.

Multiple questions

Don't be put off by multiple questions. If you can't remember each part of a question then ask for it to be repeated, or even ignore the bit you can't remember! Be prepared to use a notepad to jot down the points.

Questions that demand a long answer

If you feel a question cannot be dealt with quickly then consider deferring it until the end. This is a good idea if you believe that the rest of the audience weren't too interested either!

Hostile and emotionally charged questions

Don't meet emotion with emotion, keep your cool. It can be quite disarming to smile in the face of hostility (but don't, whatever you do, look patronising!) Certainly to be seen to be angry may cause you to lose the moral high ground. Of course, there are occasions when it is right to show your distaste with the sentiments expressed by the questioner, but always be polite.

If you are stunned

This can happen! The questioner tries to catch you out. If you are stunned, one response is to throw the question straight back, "I'm sorry, but could I ask you to repeat the question?" This can put doubt into the mind of the questioner and cause the repeated question to be less well formed. In the meantime, you have bought valuable thinking time. This technique is not one you should use too often!

Bridge from negative to positive issues

The technique here is to acknowledge the question but, as quickly as possible, bridge from negative to positive issues. Consider the following exchange.

Question – Are you still being affected by asbestos claims?

Answer - Yes, we've had problems with asbestos in the past but we have stopped using this toxic material for 30 years now and it has been replaced by a far superior material. Indeed, we now lead the world in producing this new material and I am delighted to announce we have just bought a factory in the US which will make us a truly global company.

Bridging can be done in a number of ways using such expressions as:

"The real issue is ..."

"What you *should* be asking is ..."

"It makes more sense to talk about ..."

A word of caution about bridging - use it to build a bridge to a relevant key point that is important to the questioner rather than to evade the question. When you evade a question you lose credibility (yes, politicians do it all the time but they are in a different ball game and a poor example to follow).

Rephrase the question

If questions are put to you in such a way that your answer is bound to sound defensive, a good technique is to rephrase the question on your own terms, which you then answer. Consider the exchange below.

Question - Mr Chairman, are you going to cut jobs?

Rephrasing – I understand your concern about jobs. Of course, the best way to secure jobs in the long term is to improve our profitability. Let me tell you about my 5-step plan for improving the performance of our company... **If pressed again you could say** – I really cannot be drawn on cutting jobs right now.

Seek allies

You are being questioned by an individual in a negative and hostile way and yet you know one of his colleagues agrees with your point of view. Use his colleague as your ally. "Roger, what is your view on this problem?" This may shut the other person up!

Questions seeking a "Yes/No" answer

The questioner wants you to choose between two alternatives, both of which look bad. Don't feel you have to be precise with your answer. In certain situations you can reasonably evade the question – "I can't answer that in a public forum as it is sensitive information that our competitors would love to have!"

Positive/negative questions

Question - There are many interesting points in what you are saying but ... the timing wasn't really right for the campaign to be effective, isn't that true?

This is typical. The questioner begins with something positive, in order not to come across as over-critical, but follows up with a "but". Focus your answer on the key issue - the campaign. You could say, "Yes these are a number of issues affecting the campaign. However, I believe it will prove to be successful in the end because…"

Stage management issues

With large audiences you need to consider a number of stage management issues, some of which are outlined below.

Practical points

Take questions at the end

If you allow questions at any stage of your presentation the danger is they could throw you off course. This can be particularly damaging in formal situations. In these situations, ask the audience to keep questions until the end.

In less formal situations, however, you may welcome interruptions. Even here, though, questions are not always welcome. If a question comes too early you can always compromise – give the questioner the briefest of answers but say you will return to the issue later.

Finish on time

The session is going well and you are tempted to keep going past the scheduled finish time. Don't! There may be people whose plans depend on you finishing on time. Of course, you could bring the meeting to a close in a formal sense but offer to stay behind to take more questions.

Look around

When answering questions it is natural to maintain direct eye contact with the questioner. You should, however, try to involve all the audience in your answer – look around, engage everyone's interest.

If making a team presentation

If you are making a team presentation make sure you have planned who is going to answer different types of questions or that you have a chairman. The chairman should not hog all the questions but farm some or all of them out. A good chairman might give warning to a colleague when a difficult question comes up, "I'll ask Peter to answer that one but while he is thinking of an answer I'll make a quick comment." Peter should be grateful, he is being given a little breathing space rather than being dropped in at the deep end.

If no one asks questions

It feels uncomfortable to be confronted with silence when you have asked for questions. If no one asks questions you could:

● Plant a question on the floor.
● Get the chairman to ask a question.
● Ask the audience a question, but it must be a simple one that is not intimidating.
● Frame your own question which you then answer — "One question I often get asked is …"

Quiz answers

A1.   Disagree. Answering questions is not simply about being good on your feet but also a matter of doing your homework, being brief and courteous.

A2.   Disagree. Most questioners prefer short answers as long ones can confuse.

A3.   Probably agree. By all means be helpful and friendly when answering questions, but be careful not to stray into areas you are not competent to comment on or say something you later regret!

A4.   Agree. Presenters should always anticipate questions, both friendly and hostile.

Postscript

This book has explored three areas - physical delivery, intellectual content and interactive skills. Just as few people are going to learn to fly an aeroplane or play a musical instrument from reading a book, so too should many of the ideas and skills outlined here be practised and refined in real life! However, we have written this book with a practical purpose in mind - to help presenters achieve two objectives:

- To get their message across to the audience strongly enough for the audience to be able to identify the key points and "retell the story".
- To get their personality across in terms of conviction and persuasion - "This is someone I trust."

Improving presentation skills involves a certain amount of effort - you may need to learn some new techniques, and you will certainly need to practise. Of course, if you are constantly on your feet having to speak, then your confidence will grow.

Confidence may help nerves and the perception of how you, the presenter, come across, but clarity of message is not guaranteed. Naturally gifted speakers, with quick wit and an adroit ability to think on their feet, do exist. But for most of us the ability to speak and present effectively is something we have to work at.

We have condensed all our ideas into an aide-memoire.

Aide-memoire **Physical tools**

- Make use of pauses. Pause to let the audience not only listen but also process your ideas.
- Pause to be seen to think. It's good to be seen to be thinking!
- Pause and gain eye contact at the end of an idea. This is:
  - conversational
  - engaging if done in a low key way
  - emphatic and powerful if done with deliberation.
- With a script:
  - use a combination of the Bite/Eyescan and Kissinger techniques, but don't overdo it.
- With notes:
  - write good, clear notes
  - be disciplined in following them.

Intellectual tools

- Analyse your objective/s. Why are you speaking? Is it to inform, persuade or initiate action?
- Analyse your message. What is the most important point that you wish to make and would like your audience to remember? What other points would you like your audience to remember?
- Analyse your use of language. How will you ensure your points are understood and recalled later? Will they pass the "Daisy the cow" test or merely be seen as abstract statements? Remember, abstraction is defeated by:
  - analogy
  - vivid example
  - story/case study.
- Make a strong start. Catch your audience's attention at the beginning of the presentation so that they want to listen to you and are focused on the main thrust of what you are talking about.
- Make a strong finish:
  - summarise key points
  - link any rhetoric or abstract statements to something tangible, perhaps a vivid example or case study you used earlier.

Interactive tools

- When handling questions:
  - pause to think and be seen to think
  - keep your answers short
  - be prepared to bridge from negative to positive issues.